14

P9-CEV-638

DATE DUE

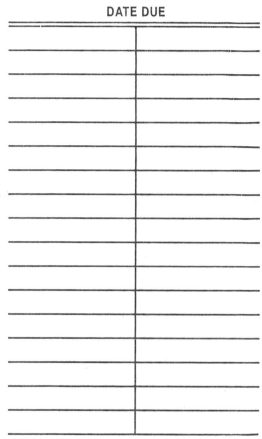

DEMCO, INC. 38-2931

THE LIBRARY OF THE WESTWARD EXPANSION™

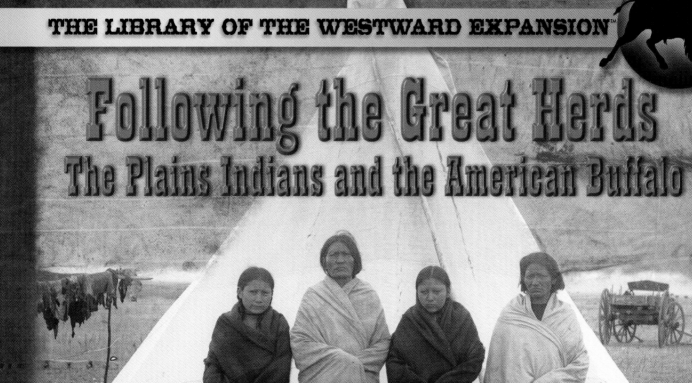

Following the Great Herds
The Plains Indians and the American Buffalo

Ryan P. Randolph

The Rosen Publishing Group's
PowerKids Press™
New York

To my wife, Joanne, thank you for everything

Published in 2003 by The Rosen Publishing Group, Inc.
29 East 21st Street, New York, NY 10010

First Edition

Managing Editor: Kathy Kuhtz Campbell
Book Design: Emily Muschinske

Photo Credits: Cover, back cover, title page, pp. 5, 9, 10, 13, 14, 17 (inset), 18 courtesy of the Denver Public Library, Western History Collection, images X-31113 (cover, back cover, title page—hide), B-790 (cover, title page), X-33703 (5), B-904 (left, 9), X-31553 (center, 9), X-33848 (right, 9), X-31726 (10), X-31968 (inset, 10), X-33708 (13), X-31702 (14), NS-2 (17), X-33806 (18), X-32338 (inset, 18); back cover (hide painting), p. 14 (inset) courtesy of Werner Forman/Art Resource, NY; p. 5 (inset), 17 © North Wind Picture Archives; p. 6 courtesy of the Northwestern University Library; p. 21 © CORBIS; p. 21 (inset) © Bettmann/CORBIS; p. 22 Fred Hultstrand History in Pictures Collection, NDIRS-NDSU, Fargo.

Randolph, Ryan P.
Following the great herds : the Plains Indians and the American Buffalo / Ryan P. Randolph.
       p. cm. — (The library of the westward expansion)
Includes bibliographical references and index.
Summary: Details the effects of westward expansion on the Plains Indian Nations, who followed the seasonal migrations of buffalo herds.
ISBN 0-8239-6296-2 (lib. bdg.)
1. Indians of North America—Hunting—Great Plains—Juvenile literature. 2. American bison—Great Plains—Juvenile literature. 3. Indians of North America—Great Plains—Migrations—Juvenile literature. [1. Indians of North America—Great Plains. 2. Bison. 3. United States—Territorial expansion.] I. Title. II. Series.
E78.G7 R36 2003
639'.11643'0978—dc21

                                    2001006967

Manufactured in the United States of America

Contents

Plains Indians Before 1492

The Plains Indians lived in the region of North America known as the Great Plains. The Plains Indians had been living in North America long before the first European explorers arrived in 1492. Signs of **nomadic** hunters and gatherers living in the area of the upper Great Plains date from 12,600 years ago. They began to develop their **cultures** and ways of life about 500 years before Christopher Columbus arrived in America in 1492.

From 1860 to 1890, the white settlers who journeyed west looking for land and for new opportunities severely tested the Plains Indians' way of life. The American buffalo, on which the Native Americans depended for food, tools, and shelter, was hunted almost to **extinction**.

Artist George Catlin made this print of Plains Indians chasing buffalo after his 1830–1836 trip through the West. Inset: The Great Plains are located west of the Mississippi River and east of the Rocky Mountains, and they stretch north into Canada and south into Texas.

The Great Plains

THE NEW WEST
AS IT IS.

SCALE OF MILES
0   100   200   300   400   500

Where the Buffalo Roam

The Plains Indians' main source of food, tools, clothing, and shelter was the American buffalo. Buffalo probably came from Asia over the **Bering land bridge** that connected Siberia with Alaska during **prehistoric** times. The ancestors of the Plains Indians probably followed the buffalo from Siberia to the Great Plains. The region of the Great Plains was a very good place for buffalo to live because there was a lot of food and there were not many natural enemies. The Plains Indians killed very few buffalo, and the only other major threats to buffalo were blizzards, rainstorms, and **prairie** fires.

Edward S. Curtis took this photograph of buffalo on the Great Plains around 1927. It is believed that before the 1800s, four great herds of millions of buffalo each roamed the Great Plains.

DID YOU KNOW?

The animal we call buffalo in America is not really a buffalo but a bison. We often use the words *buffalo* and *bison* to describe the same animal.

The Nations of the Plains Indians

Many Native American nations make up the group known as the Plains Indians. The main nations are the Sioux, Cheyenne, Arapaho, Comanche, Crow, and Kiowa. The name *Sioux* refers to a group of people who spoke a common language. Several groups made up the Sioux. The Santee Sioux were the easternmost Sioux people and lived in the woodlands of today's Minnesota. The Lakota Sioux, also known as the Teton Sioux, lived farther west. Several groups made up the Teton Sioux, including the Oglala Sioux and the Hunkpapa Sioux. The Cheyenne and the Arapaho lived farther east in Minnesota, but they **migrated** west as white settlers moved to the area. The northern Cheyenne were allies, or friends, of the Sioux and lived in the area of today's Montana and Wyoming. The southern Cheyenne lived on the plains of Kansas and Colorado.

Right: *A Hunkpapa chief is covered in buffalo hide that has been decorated.* Middle: *A Santee Sioux chief's son wears a headdress, or decoration for the head, and sits on a buffalo hide.* Far Right: *A Ute woman wears beaded moccasins and a frontier-style dress.*

Life on the Great Plains

The Great Plains was made up of either flatlands or rolling hills covered with much prairie grass but few trees. Summers were hot, and winters were cold and harsh. Plains Indians got their food by hunting animals, by fishing, by gathering berries and other fruit, or by farming maize, a special kind of corn.

Some Plains Indians, such as the Teton Sioux and the Cheyenne, were nomadic. They moved their villages to follow the animals they hunted, such as buffalo and antelope. Others, such as the Santee Sioux, remained in one area, living near rivers or streams to fish or to farm the lands.

Santee Sioux tepees, or shelters, are shown in this 1871 photograph. The Plains Indians often decorated tepees with religious paintings. Inset: The Plains Indians used buffalo skins as robes.

DID YOU KNOW?

A buffalo can weigh up to 2,000 pounds (907 kg), can be 12 feet (4 m) long, and more than 6 feet (2 m) tall at its hump, the big lump over its shoulders. It can run up to 40 miles per hour (64 km/h) for farther than 100 yards (91 m).

11

The Buffalo Hunt

The Plains Indians used different methods to hunt buffalo. Before they had horses, bands of hunters separated small groups of buffalo from the larger herds and killed the animals using bows and arrows. Sometimes a group of hunters scared the buffalo to make them run over a cliff. At the bottom of the cliff, the women would then skin and cut up the dead buffalo, so that the buffalo could be taken back to the hunters' village.

In the 1500s, the first Spanish explorers **introduced** horses to Native Americans. After the Pueblos fought the Spaniards in 1680, the Pueblos began to raise horses and to trade them with the Kiowa and the Comanche. Hunting buffalo became easier for Native Americans as they became expert horsemen. Riding horses made it easier for nomadic Plains Indians to pack up their villages and follow the roaming herds of buffalo.

Top: *Riding their horses, the Plains Indians chased the buffalo and shot arrows as the herd tried to run away.* Bottom: *The print* Buffalo Hunt under the White Wolf Skin *shows Plains Indians using wolf skins to sneak up on buffalo so that they could kill them.*

Leaving Very Little to Waste

The Plains Indians killed only as many buffalo as they needed. After the hunters killed a group of buffalo, the women and men who did not hunt removed each buffalo's skin. They placed the buffalo meat and organs in the skin, and they put the bones on top. The package was put in a **travois**, which a horse or dog pulled back to the village.

Plains Indians ate the meat of the buffalo. They used the hide to make clothes, shields, and tepees, the cone-shaped shelters in which Plains Indians lived. The Plains Indians could easily put up or take down tepees, so they were ideal shelters for people on the move.

In this 1878 photo, buffalo hides have been stacked in a Sioux village in Montana. The Plains Indians used all parts of a buffalo. They used the hides for tepees, the bones as tools, and the tail as a whip or a fly swatter. They made the horns into children's toys or cups. Inset: This Shoshone painting on buffalo hide shows a buffalo dance after a hunt.

DID YOU KNOW?

Most Plains Indians believed that the Spirits created life and controlled all animals and plants. They thought of the buffalo as a sacred, or religious, animal, because it provided them with food, tools, shelter, and clothes.

The Coming of the White Settlers

The Plains Indians had met white explorers, hunters, and fur trappers for years before the Louisiana Purchase in 1803. In the 1820s, white settlers began to move west. They traveled on the Santa Fe Trail in 1821, and the Oregon Trail in 1843. With the discovery of gold in California in 1848, people rushed to the West to strike it rich. Settlers crossing the Great Plains passed through the Plains Indians' lands. In 1851, the Sioux, Arapaho, and Cheyenne made a **treaty** with the U.S. government at Fort Laramie, in Wyoming. The government agreed to pay the Plains Indians $50,000 per year for the right to build forts and roads across their lands. In the 1860s and the 1870s, gold was found in Colorado and South Dakota, and railroads were built in the West. The settlers soon broke the treaty and forced the Plains Indians out of their hunting grounds and land.

White hunters shoot buffalo during a Wild West show in the 1880s. Inset: Marksman William "Doc" Carver called himself the Evil Spirit of the Plains, because he said he once shot a white buffalo. The Sioux believe that a white buffalo is a sacred animal, and that only an evil spirit would kill one.

"Evil Spirit"

Right: *The only child saved from the Sand Creek Massacre was this Arapaho girl. She is seen in a photo taken about 10 years after the battle.*

Sand Creek

Sand Pits

War on the Great Plains

As whites settled in Native American lands, **tensions** rose and many settlers, soldiers, and Plains Indians killed one another. In 1864, at the Sand Creek **Massacre** in Colorado, Black Kettle and the Cheyenne, who were promised safety, were instead killed by the **3rd Colorado Volunteers**. Tensions between Native Americans and white settlers grew with the opening of cattle trails, such as the Bozeman Trail. In 1868, the Cheyenne, the Sioux, and the U.S. government made a second treaty at Fort Laramie. However, it was soon broken in 1874, when miners found gold in the Black Hills of South Dakota.

Far Left: This 1864 drawing shows the locations of the Cheyenne tepees and the 3rd Colorado Volunteers at the battle at Sand Creek. About 28 Plains Indian men and 105 Plains Indian women and children died during the battle.

DID YOU KNOW?

The Plains Indians fought white settlers who tried to mine sacred lands. The fighting reached its peak in 1876, at the Battle of Little Bighorn in Montana, when the Sioux and Cheyenne killed General George A. Custer and his troops.

White Hunters of Buffalo

Although the U.S. Army and the plans of the U.S. government helped to destroy the Plains Indians' way of life, the mass killing of the buffalo also played a big part. The number of buffalo that roamed the Great Plains before 1867 was 25 million at the peak. In 1870, the number was cut to about 5 million. White hunters killed buffalo for the meat and the hides. The Army hired these hunters to supply troops with meat. The railroad companies also hired white hunters to supply meat to the workers who laid tracks. Most of the buffalo were killed for their hides. In 1872 and 1873, 1.5 million buffalo hides were shipped east to make robes and coats. After killing the buffalo, the white hunters skinned the animals where they fell and left the meat to rot. People traveling west often described in their diaries the bad smell of the rotting flesh and the sight of the bones that littered the plains.

A buffalo-hide yard in Dodge City, Kansas, shows stacks of about 40,000 hides. In the 1870s, some leather companies paid hunters $3 for each hide. Inset: It is said that William "Buffalo Bill" Cody killed 4,000 buffalo in just two years.

As the numbers of buffalo killed for their hides grew, wasteful killing of buffalo began to rise. One of the most wasteful ways was for railroad passengers to shoot buffalo from the windows of a moving train. The buffalo they shot and killed were just left on the plains to rot. By 1897, the number of American buffalo that existed was very small. There were only about 20 buffalo in Yellowstone National Park. However, careful protection and preservation saved the buffalo from extinction. Today many buffalo live in national parks, such as Yellowstone.

The Ghost Dance

In 1889, a Paiute holy man named Wovoka had a vision that led to the Ghost Dance movement. The Ghost Dance was believed to **reunite** those who joined in it with their friends and relatives in the ghost world. People who believed in the Ghost Dance claimed that whites would disappear and that the great herds of buffalo would return to the Great Plains. The Ghost Dance caused fear among whites. This fear resulted in the massacre of about 300 Native American men, women, and children by the U.S. Army at Wounded Knee Creek in South Dakota in December 1890. Today the massacre at Wounded Knee sadly represents the end of freedom for the Plains Indians and their way of life.

In 1907, the last buffalo in North Dakota was killed.

Glossary

Bering land bridge (BAYR-ing LAND BRIJ) The strip of land that at one time formed a bridge or means of crossing from Siberia to Alaska, where the Bering Strait is today.

cultures (KUL-churz) The beliefs, art, behaviors, customs, and social activities of groups of people.

extinction (ik-STINK-shun) No longer existing. This term usually refers to plant or animal species that die out or are killed off completely.

introduced (in-truh-DOOSD) To have brought into use, knowledge, or notice.

massacre (MAS-uh-ker) A fight in which many people on one side are killed.

migrated (MY-grayt-ed) To have moved from one place to another.

nomadic (no-MA-dik) Relating to nomads or to wandering from place to place with no set home. Nomads are people who wander from place to place looking for food for themselves or their animals.

prairie (PRAYR-ee) A large grassy land that can be flat or hilly.

prehistoric (pree-his-TOR-ik) Existing in times before written history.

reunite (ree-yoo-NYT) To join together again after being apart.

tensions (TEN-shunz) Pressure or strain between two groups of people or things.

3rd Colorado Volunteers (THURD kah-luh-RAH-doh vah-luhn-TEERZ) The group of Colorado soldiers who offered to join the army without being asked. They were led by Colonel John Chivington at the Sand Creek Massacre on November 29, 1864.

travois (truh-VOY) A simple sled used by Plains Indians that is made of two long, trailing poles with a net or platform for carrying a load and that is pulled by a dog or a horse.

treaty (TREE-tee) An agreement made and signed by two or more groups or governments.

Index

Primary Sources

Cover and title page (back). *Buffalo Hide.* This painted and quill-worked buffalo hide was created by the Piegan (Blackfoot) tribe sometime between 1900 and 1920. It has four rows of banded quill work above some uncompleted outlines. The hide was collected by Maximilian, Prinz zu Wied, a German traveler who wrote about his trip to North America (1838–1841). **(front).** *Sitting Bull's Family.* Dakota chief Sitting Bull's two wives and daughters and one unidentified little boy pose outside a tepee during the 1880s. The photo was taken by David F. Barry (1854–1934), a Wisconsin photographer, who, over a period of 30 years, took portraits of Native Americans. **Page 5.** *Buffalo Hunt, Chase.* This print is from George Catlin's "North American Indian Portfolio." Catlin traveled in the West in the 1830s, and drew and painted many images of Native Americans on the Great Plains, including this one. **Page 6.** *As it Was in the Old Days.* Photographer Edward S. Curtis (1868–1952) included this image in *The North American Indian,* Volume 19. In 1900, Curtis began a 30-year project to document Native Americans and their lives in North America and visited more than 80 different nations. **Page 9 (left).** *Gall, Dakota Chief.* Photographer David F. Barry took this three-quarter view of Gall in his Wisconsin studio around 1881. Gall, also called Pizi, became Sitting Bull's military chief, and at the Battle of the Little Bighorn in 1876, he led Hunkpapa warriors. **(middle).** *Ma-za-oo-me (Little Bird Hunter).* This photo of a Santee Sioux chief's son was taken in 1871. **(right).** *A Native American Woman.* This photo of a Ute woman was taken between 1880 and 1900. **Page 13 (top).** *Buffalo Hunt.* Catlin included this print of Plains Indians hunters surrounding a herd of buffalo in the "North American Indian Portfolio." **(bottom).** *Buffalo Hunt Under the White Wolf Skin.* This print by George Catlin was included in the more than 40,000 photographs and prints that he reproduced in "North American Indian Portfolio." **Page 14.** *Sioux Village.* This 1878 photo of a Sioux camp in winter near Yellowstone was published by L. A. Huffman of Miles City, Montana. **(inset and back cover).** *Hide Painting.* This painting on buffalo hide shows a buffalo dance after the hunt. Thought to be a Shoshone painting, the hide is now at the Plains Indian Museum, Buffalo Bill Historical Center, Cody, Wyoming.

Web Sites

Due to the changing nature of Internet links, PowerKids Press has developed an online list of Web sites related to the subject of this book. This site is updated regularly. Please use this link to access the list:

www.powerkidslinks.com/lwe/grherd/